We Are With You, We Love You

SPIRIT PROTECTORS AND GUARDIANS

Janet Miller

We Are with You, We Love You: Spirit Protectors and Guardians
Published by JaniLyn Publishing
Bozeman, Montana

ISBN: 979-8-9916531-0-7 (Hardcover), 979-8-9916531-1-4 (Paperback)
BODY, MIND & SPIRIT / Angels & Spirit Guides, ART / Individual Artists / Artists' Books
Cataloging-in-Publication Data available

Cover and interior design by Victoria Wolf, wolfdesignandmarketing.com.

Information on the frequency of color and morphic energy can be found in Michelle Walling's "Energetic Anatomy—A Complete Guide to the Human Energy Fields and Etheric Bodies," *How to Exit the Matrix*, December 8, 2017, https://tinyurl.com/yf7rfk3s.

Author Note

This publication is for entertainment purposes only. While the publisher and author have used their best efforts in preparing this book, they make no representations or warranties with respect to the accuracy or completeness of the contents of this book and specifically disclaim any implied warranties of fitness for a particular purpose.

The advice and strategies contained herein may not be suitable for your situation. You should consult with a professional when appropriate. Neither the publisher nor the author shall be liable for any loss of profit or any other commercial damages, including but not limited to special, incidental, consequential, personal, or other damages. For privacy reasons, some names, locations, and dates may have been changed.

Contents

Welcome 1

My Journey as an Artist 3

Seeing Beyond 7

What You May Find 11

The Role of Color 13

Meet Soul Friends 17

Soul Fire 19

Soul Mates 25

Smiling Sage 29

Empresses 33

Green Guy 37

Bright Eyes 41

Women of the World 45

Angel Mountain 49

Butterflies and Kisses 53

Jeweled Life 59

Ancestors 63

Nebula Bear 67

Twins 71

Transformation/Ant Man 75

Energy of a Space 79

Winged Dragon 83

Spotted Warriors 87

Bound Hearts 91

A Bridge to the Other 95

Struggles 101

Roots and Wings 105

Spirit Mountain 109

Marilyn Monroe/Representations
of Spirit 115

Purple Sage 119

Taking Flight One 123

Taking Flight Two 127

Animal Spirit 131

Accidental Angels 139

Intuition 145

Emergence / What's Under
the Bed? 149

Little Owl / Resilience 153

The Kaleidoscope 157

Colorful One 160

Colorful Two 161

Block Original 163

Block Turtle 165

Blocks Dog 167

Blue Eyes 169

Acknowledgments 171

About the Artist 173

Welcome ...

To those who seek beauty; to those who are curious about nonphysical consciousness; to those who want to live their lives more deeply.

Welcome to a world of color and shape; to a world of meaning, if you let yourself find it; to deeper layers of the Self and the world around you.

I had no idea what I would find when I began my personal creative journey. I began painting because of a need for self-expression, and what I uncovered has enriched my life in many more ways.

I invite you on a tour of joy and of discovery. Art is more than something pretty to hang on your wall or put on your shelf. The more you look at it, the more you see. At different stages of your life, you may see different things. We are always in a process of evolution, discovery, and learning.

Art opens doors we may not have known were there.

Walk through the door with me ...

My Journey as an Artist

THE ART IN THIS BOOK ORIGINATED AFTER I was an art supply collector for years. I love art supplies! Maybe my satisfaction came from getting new school supplies as a child and filling that book bag before the first day of school: the new pencils and a new pencil box with fresh erasers. Receiving a new box of sixty-four crayons—reading and learning the names of all those beautiful colors; the sharpener in the back of the box, to keep them neat and sharp … I simply loved the anticipation of it all.

Since then, I have acquired all kinds of paints and drawing utensils, paper for painting and drawing, and charcoals and pastels, which I have yet to play with.

When I became an interior designer, I was able to use and play with many colors, textures, rulers, and erasers in my training and career.

After my training and while working on people's homes, I realized there was more at play than simply placing furniture, moving walls, and hanging drapery. Winston

Churchill famously said, "We shape our buildings and afterward our buildings shape us." My work was shaping the lives of the people who lived there.

I found myself in Mexico at a retreat with a friend and met a woman who introduced me to energy healing in the form of Reiki practice. I came away from the retreat with new information. There is a field of energy around us and in us called the etheric field, created from our body's electromagnetic charge. We are essentially a battery. As a result of our thoughts, emotions, and health, this field can become contracted and dark, and our dis-ease can turn into disease if not addressed at this stage. This energy field is affected by the vibrations we create through our emotions and the people and places around us, as well as the life experiences we hang on to. Everything is frequency, and we have either a resonance or dis-resonance (disharmony) based on thoughts and feelings. Anger, hurt, and all of those negative human emotions distract us and keep us from being present. Reiki showed the frequency of love, the loving spirit of God, my inner universe, and how it can positively influence and attune a body, reminding it of its ability to heal. Not only are we frequency emitters, but we are also frequency meters to others' energy.

This knowledge helped me move through what I was going through at the time. Simply through the energy I was receiving through the Reiki provider from Source and my body's ability to heal itself, I could feel myself come back to my center again, which gave me relief from the pain I was feeling. The experience was such a wonderful relief. I wanted more!

Then came my study of Feng Shui, which includes the Bagua Map. The Bagua represent different aspects of life, such as wealth, health, relationships, and career. I hoped to bring together the frequency of the chakras, the frequency and elements of the Baguas, and color healing and psychology in the spaces my clients lived and worked in.

I was raised in a Christian home in the Midwest and went to a Christian day school for my first eight years, learning and reciting Bible passages, songs, and stories. The concepts I learned as an adult profoundly changed the way I thought about myself, my place in the world, and the place of my creativity. The different teachings didn't conflict in my mind, but rather dovetailed in my understanding and made everything come together. I believe God is my Father, and as I am His child, He wants the best for me, just as any good father does. He wants me to use my God-given gifts in this life.

The urge to pick up my paintbrush and slather paint on a paper using just the passion I was feeling became more than I could hold back. I didn't collect art supplies any longer; I *used* them.

Seeing Beyond

THE PAINTING, *Soul Fire*, seen on page 19 reflects my transformation. The colors show the intensity of what I was feeling. There is a figure in *Soul Fire* that appears to be on fire, not in a negative way, but rather in a passionate expression.

Then came *Soul Mates*.

As a design student, an art instructor had told me that my talents lent themselves to being a fabric designer. After I began painting, my daughter uploaded my paintings to a site that created fabrics from people's art. The process involved mirroring my work, which resulted in a design with greater depth and a completely different viewing experience than my originals.

Looking at the results, my daughter observed, "There are always some dudes in your paintings …"

When I say "mirrored version," think of a mountain lake reflecting the sky and the mountains. The landscape is "upside down" relative to its reflection.

Where the original and its reflection come together is where I began seeing figures or images that I now call "soul friends."

Taking a closer look, I could see what my daughter meant. When *Soul Mates* is mirrored with its own image, a set of characters appears as a totem in the center of the new art. As I created more paintings and mirrored those images, I saw these figures in most of my works. *Soul Mates* made it difficult to deny there was something going on in the paintings. I had no intention or ability to create the characters that showed up in the mirrored version.

Sometimes, these characters also show up in the original, before I mirror it. I don't always see them initially, but suddenly, I discover a new surprise. *Hello! There you are!*

The appearance of these images confused me at first, so I decided to use the practice of accessing my Higher Self by putting a pen in my dominant hand to ask a question, and switching to my nondominant hand to answer with what came to my mind. I asked what I needed to do with my art, where the figures came from, and why they began to appear in my work, and why they looked the way they did.

The experiment turned into something more than I expected.

In my spirit inquiry, it was conveyed to me concerning these images and the force that created them: "We are not souls but energetic representations of spirit, and warriors and protectors from past lives." They are here with us and love us, they said. They are neither good nor evil but spirits of love and divine embodiment (or possibly disembodiment) of hope for people on Earth. When I asked if they were alien, they told me they are indeed alien to some who have never experienced such wonderful feelings and energy. They are conscious awareness, holding love as a goal for this world and universe.

They want to show us what is inside us all, and how through persevering and listening to that small, quiet voice of our soul and Higher Self, what we can achieve.

What I believe is being shown to me in my art is the secret forces at play within and around us. I am seeing the wisdom of nature and the animal world being worked on by the spirit world to give us messages about where we are on our path and what we came here to do. Each of our souls has characteristics that make us unique, and each of us is on a special and significant journey.

I believe the nonphysical consciousness at play in our lives includes angels, ancestors, and aspects or energies of our personalities. Aspects of our spiritual natures as well as our past experiences. Our bodies and emotions, as illustrated in **Bound Hearts**. The galaxy and earth energies, as explored in **Nebula Bear** and **Women of the World**.

I see a lot of the Divine showing itself in these pieces—aspects of beauty and love these angels and spirits have for us, and the good intentions they have for our lives, if we only knew what we are capable of and tapped into it. They are there for us when we need them, if we would only ask. God gave us our own guardian angels.

Psalms 91:11 (New International Version):

For he will command his angels concerning you to guard you in all your ways.

Many soul friends are representations of the spirit of the person, place, or thing they're attached to. They share or embody a piece of myself or the person for whom the painting was created. I find whoever sees these paintings usually finds some aspect or painting they resonate with as well.

When I embark on a painting, I meditate. When I close my eyes, I see something like the aurora borealis. I put those waves of color on the canvas, and it becomes the background.

What You May Find

YOU MAY FIND TOTEMS OF BEARS, spiders, phoenixes, priests, a sage sitting under a tree with a fire on his head, and spacemen in the paintings. Perhaps baboons, bats, wolves, buffalo, and many more soul friends. Even the dark energy I captured after an office space I was in felt very uncomfortable.

These animals, birds, or reptiles each have a different significance, depending on the personality and characteristics of that animal. Each animal has a secret life, an agenda of sorts, and the ways nature works through them are likewise distinct and varied. Each have a story to tell. If we stop and reflect, their spirits speak to us. It's interesting to look up and see the animal's symbolic meaning. Are they metaphors for what Spirit is trying to convey to us?

Because of my Christian upbringing, what I sometimes see I decipher from that perspective.

It seems to me to all be interrelated. There is wisdom out there to be tapped into. We just need to listen, watch, and observe what's being revealed to us.

You may also notice a dreamlike quality to some of the images showing up. They are images that we only recognize by the personalities they are emanating. There are characters in our dreams that we don't recognize in our waking worlds, yet who can provide meaning for us.

All of this is part of our soul's path. These characters represent us and are being communicated through the art in a way that our guides think we will understand. They see us and the gifts and strengths we have brought to this life, as well as what we're being challenged to overcome or grow from.

As my question-and-answer practice told me, deciding what you see is up to you.

The Role of Color

DID YOU KNOW THE EFFECT COLOR, or the lack of it in your environment, can have on your life?

Imagine going into your closet every morning and seeing only one color to put on every day. Would that color truly express who you are and what you are feeling that day or the image you want to portray to the world?

Think of the red power tie that you put on to perhaps give yourself a little more confidence, or the cool blue jeans that you slip on when you want to relax. Essentially, you are medicating yourself for a desired feeling or effect with color.

I think it is important to note here that I'm applying the feeling of the color to the frequency it relates to. Each color of the rainbow is related to a frequency. Below are the frequencies that have been measured in the human energy field by Dr. Valerie *Hunt in A Study of Structural Neuromuscular, Energy Field, and Emotional Approaches.*

Blue 250–275 Hz plus 1,200 Hz

Green 250–475 Hz

Yellow 500–700 Hz

Orange 950–1050 Hz

Red 1,000–1,200 Hz

Violet 1,000–2,000, plus 300–400; 600–800 Hz

White 1,100–2,000 Hz

Interior design, Reiki, and Feng Shui all understand colors to have a deeper meaning. Interior design taught me the psychology of color and its effect on the inhabitants of a space. Energy healing, or Reiki, uses the concept of the body's chakras, each of which is associated with certain colors. Likewise in the Bagua, each element and color plays a role in creating energetic balance in a space. Those frequencies will align us in various ways or can be used as a Feng Shui cure to enhance our spaces.

In Reiki, we use the chakras and related colors to heal with visualization. In Feng Shui, we use color in the space we're working on. In color therapy, we breathe in a color that speaks to us, in slow breaths, feeling the color fill our entire body; the color healing whatever condition we want to balance and correct.

I believe we do ourselves a great disservice by removing color from our home environments. We know how personal colors can be. If someone has a strong reaction to a color, it's a big clue to me of what might be going on with the person and what action or inquiry to make to help balance them out again. Art is a great way to introduce color into your life.

We have seen so much in recent times linking frequency to healing, be it ultraviolet or a red laser. Why wouldn't it be conceivable for every color of the rainbow in between to be just as important for us?

Why not use color to have the effect you choose for your life?

Meet Soul Friends

SOME OF MY ART AROSE ONLY FROM the desire to paint; some pieces I created with others in mind, showing their soul friends. I call these "soul paintings."

There is more to us than we realize. I'm excited for you to discover what you see and what it means to you.

Soul Fire

OIL ON ART PAPER

I see a fiery spirit with its arms outstretched and its hips wrapped in cloth. It is burning with intensity but in a way that releases a long-held tension and desire to create.

I didn't know what I would paint when I began; I simply connected with the use of the colors and the freedom to express what I felt inside. And I surrendered to the urges I was getting from my spirit. In the image, which is mirrored four times, you will see what looks like two gargoyle figures. Historically, gargoyles were called "grotesques." They were protectors of a building and meant to ward off evil spirits. It appears evil spirits are being warded off here, too.

Red represents the first chakra. In Western philosophy, different chakras are associated with different colors of the rainbow. This chakra and color are connected to the foundation for our lives: our family of origin, and having enough to care for daily needs. Whether supportive and nurturing or turbulent, our first life lesson will continue to haunt us, unless we embrace it for what it was and the lessons it taught us. Is there more than one way to see your experience? Is there a version which would soften its impact on you?

Green is connected to the heart chakra. All experiences in the lower chakras, when filtered through our heart's compassion (the fourth chakra), create compassion for the people and experiences in those early years. *Soul Fire* represents a release from what was holding me back.

Soul Mates

OIL ON ART PAPER

This was one of the first paintings I did. I enjoy the background creation. The stickman with a heart was something I just felt like painting at the time.

Little did I know the soul friends who would show up once I mirrored this piece. I've enjoyed deciphering each and every one and their spiritual meaning. From the silly little creature on top of the totem to the deer or bear above him. I see watchful human eyes, a rodent, a warrior with a helmet on his knees, a spaceman with an oxygen hose around his neck, a creative spider, and another little cat on top of an owl.

Sometimes, we overlook, subdue, and repress the powerful force within us, a part of our being, yet distinct as its own entity, longing to be expressed. We know there is something there, but how do we access it? We must listen to our deepest nature. Follow your heart song …

Smiling Sage

INK ON RAW CANVAS

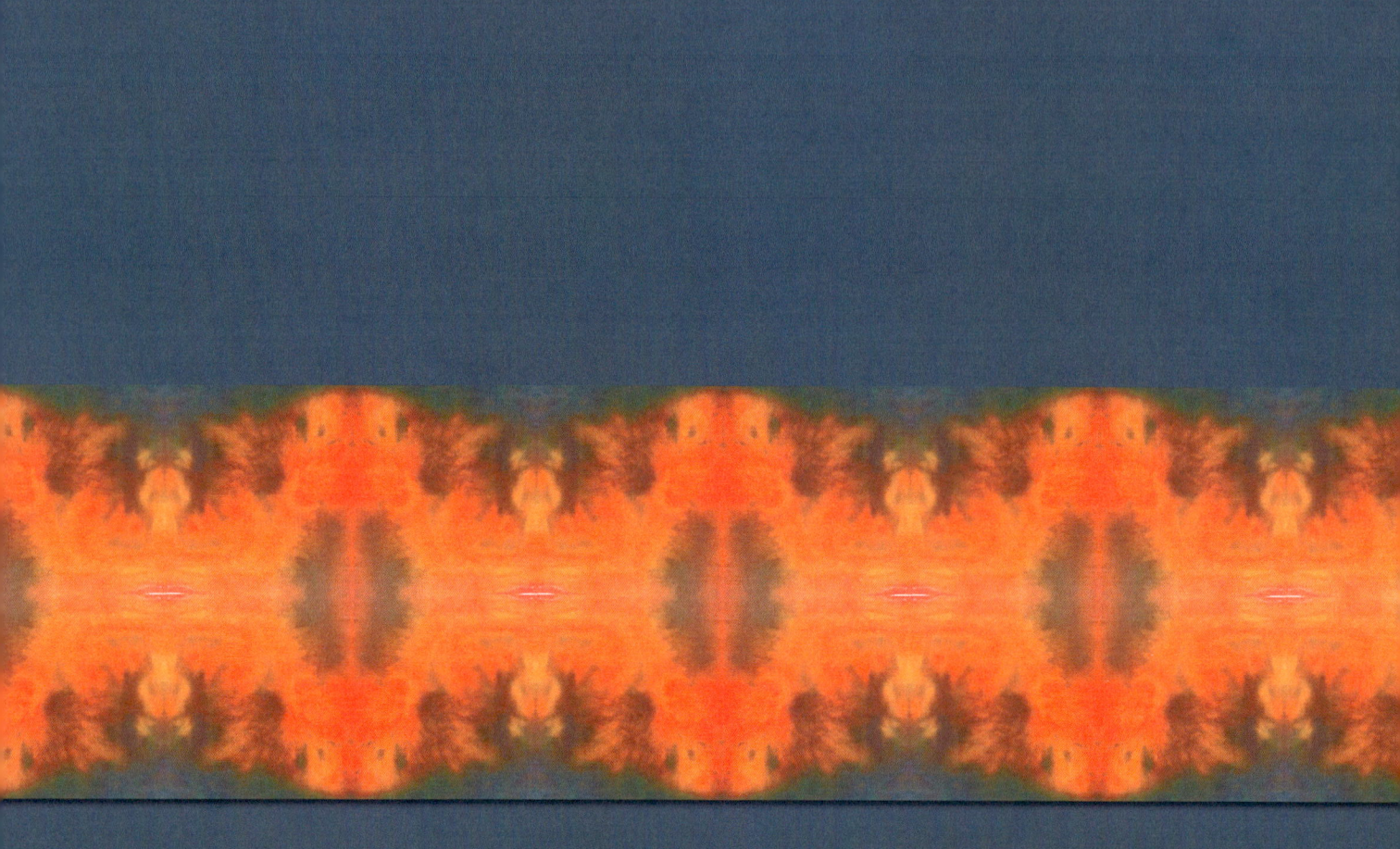

I mirrored this colorful piece two times to reveal its message to us. It would have lost its message if I had fixed the upper right corner and filled it in, thereby squaring the painting. Sometimes, it's good not to be a perfectionist.

Whether you see a smile emanating from this being, an opening in the fabric of space and time, a larger smiling face with glowing hair, or something else is entirely appropriate.

Empresses

INK ON FOAM CORE

Empresses came about somewhat by accident; it was originally just foam core protecting my table while I painted another piece. I liked the outcome, so I mirrored it and discovered a small girl standing on a gem with a castle or some kind of building on her head. Mirroring the image to the sides is another story. I see three characters. The middle one has a reptilian look about it and is standing very straight and proper.

What do you see?

Green Guy

OIL ON ART PAPER

I experimented with multiple techniques in this painting, applying oil to art paper and using a scraping tool to create various patterns. I thought, *Hmmm, no dudes in this one*. It was only later, while talking on the phone and viewing it from a particular angle, that I noticed the Green Guy with his silly smile looking back at me. Can you see him, too?

Bright Eyes

OIL ON CANVAS

I started playing with this painting, and
the eyes are now layered under another
one. Sometimes the most difficult thing
as an artist is to know when to stop.

I love these eyes! They seem very clear and healthy. The pastel colors create a friendly, gentle energy. The characters who showed up in the middle have a story to tell as well.

Women of the World

WATERCOLOR ON ART PAPER

46

While watching the news, I saw sizzling lava flowing from a Hawaiian volcano, creating a plume of steam as it hit the ocean. Seeing this had a big impact on me. The painting, created a couple of days later, showed the message it had for me.

In the original, I see a kneeling woman who, like the Earth, has a flow and a connection to the push and pull of nature on her body. Mirrored, I see women bleed for the four corners of the Earth.

Like Mother Earth, women are built to be nurturers and can also be a force to be reckoned with. The Earth is continually trying to take herself back from any human-made creations, as our bodies are continually healing themselves from the unnatural creations we inflict on them. We, as women, nurture our families, as Earth supports and nurtures us. The figure I see is in tune with the Earth and humanity.

Angel Mountain

WATERCOLOR ON ART PAPER

I felt the need to bring something into the world that was bubbling inside me. As usual, I would never have predicted what would be expressed through this painting; I just let my intuition play. What comes out of this practice never fails to surprise and sometimes amuse me. It's like deciphering a dream.

What I see in the painting is a mountain—an important element in Feng Shui. This type of mountain relates to money generation and stability. I also see a figure wearing a crown, which is traditionally associated with power and dignity. This figure is holding up an angel in the sky. The angel represents divine love and protection. What's under the angel and crowned figure in the mountain? A manger. What's the meaning of the manger? The Christ child is accessible to everyone.

What is important to notice are the figures of two different modalities: Christianity and Feng Shui.

In the reversed position, there is a totally different character who seems to be wearing a tutu or dance outfit. I don't have a good explanation for that one!

Butterflies and Kisses

ACRYLIC ON ART PAPER

These rather luxurious colors remind me of velvet and royalty. Magenta is an overall balancing color for all the chakras. If you have only one color to use and meditate on, this would be it.

When mirrored, we find a butterfly uplifting the entire image. Turned sideways, I see playful eyes with the hand mudra, which represents love. The X in the center becomes the body of a character with a pleasant demeanor. The spiritual meaning of X is a representation of balance and unity within yourself or the world around you.

Jeweled Life

WATERCOLOR ON ART PAPER

This mirrored version seems to have two power sources. Notice the serious, strong-looking character highlighted in the separate image, a lioness with an elephant at its third eye. Elephants relate to wisdom, strength, and spirituality. What looks like a female lion would represent fierce protection, standing her ground, being courageous as well as nurturing, and working as a team as a pride of lions would.

Ancestors

OIL ON CANVAS

After completing this painting, I recognized a familiar face among the others. In the upper right corner, there's a gentleman with a white mustache. I went searching and found images of my paternal and maternal grandfathers. Both had passed away before I was born. I feel as though this work is a message from my ancestors, acknowledging me even though I never had the chance to know them.

As for the other characters, they reveal family pain and various personalities that are undoubtedly also part of my DNA. This seems to be telling me we carry with us the energy of past generations. It's up to us to heal what was passed on to us through all time and space, even though we had nothing to do with its creation. Is this what's referred to as morphic energy? I'm intrigued by the scientist Rupert Sheldrake's philosophy that past–life memories can move between lifetimes through a soul's morphic energy field. Morphic energy fields are how a cell knows what part of the body to create in utero. Whether it should make a heart or an eye. It's how gifts of a grandparent may be passed onto a grandchild, such as math ability or musical knowledge. Is that where the belief in multiple lifetimes comes from? Memories passed on in this way?

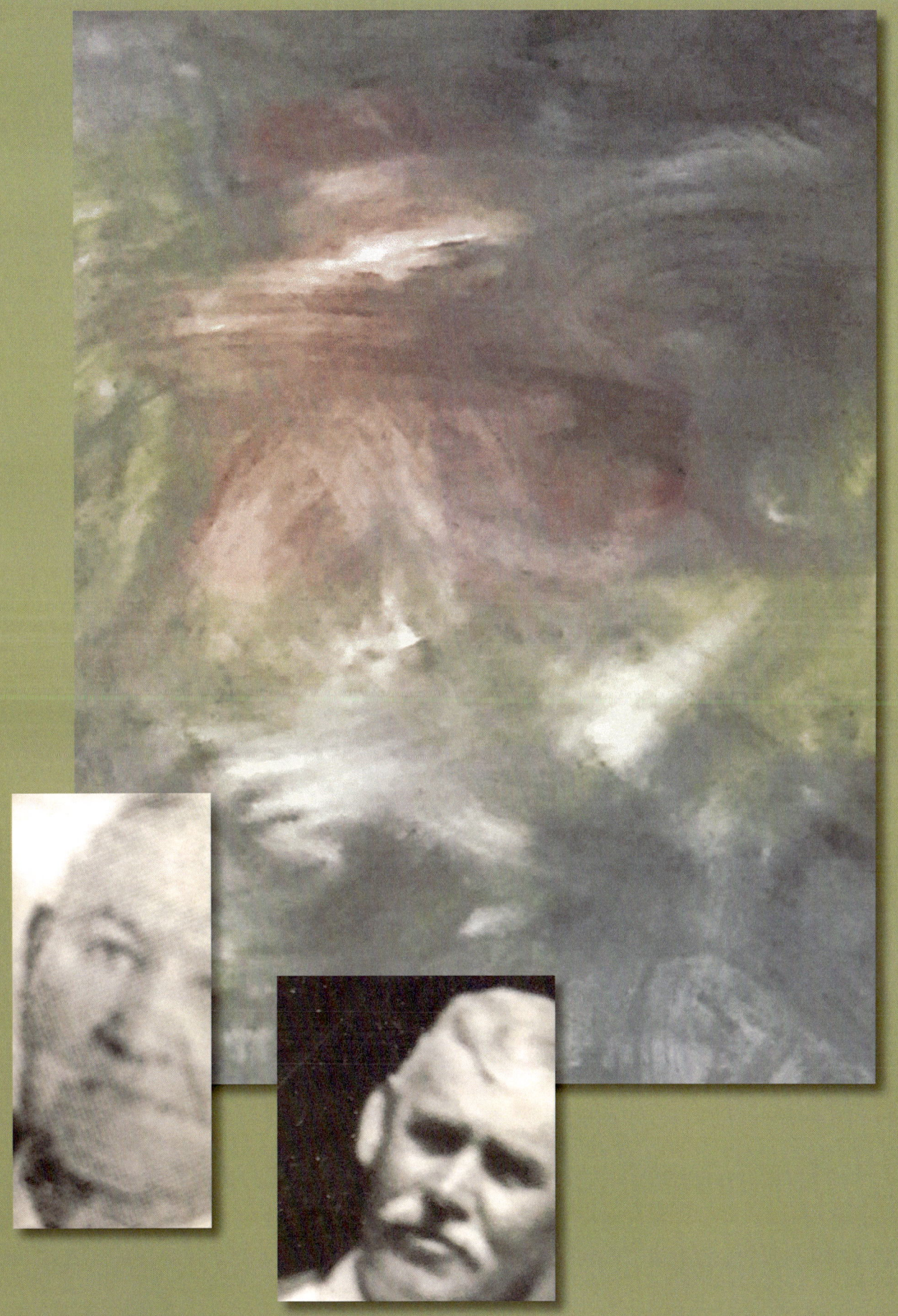

Nebula Bear

WATERCOLOR ON ART PAPER

After painting an image replicating what
I saw in meditation, I mirrored it and saw
what I interpreted as a bear, a powerful
guide. A few days later, I saw a picture of
a nebula, which had the same colors and
shape and spirit of a bear.

Is this what they wanted to show me
in the meditation? Was the Bear Spirit
telling me to stand tall, grasp life, and to
be fearless? Or perhaps that I needed
cave time and to go deep within?
It made me think that this guiding
consciousness travels in those places in
the universe.

Twins

WATERCOLOR ON ART PAPER

I see crab people. I don't know if there is such a thing, but as a spirit protector, the crab represents changing course and heading in a new direction. This mirrored version definitely creates a twin with the third chakra, yellow in this case (ego), between them. I see two obvious beings with smiling faces, and then, upon further investigation, there are the two crab-like creatures at the bottom. The part I really love is right above the purple hair at the top of the painting: a closed-eye face I have highlighted in a separate image.What does your intuition tell you?

Transformation/Ant Man

ACRYLIC ON ART PAPER

This painting was a surprise, as usual. In interpreting this piece, I delved into the fascinating world of Ant People and Hopi folklore, as well as the symbolism of ants as guiding entities. Ant People were said to be crucial in Hopi survival.

The image shows an enlightened third eye. Magenta is an overall balancing color for the body; the color pink relates to the heart chakra. The yellow is vibrant and relates to the third chakra: ego, personal power, self-esteem, and getting things done, just like ants who are hard workers, strong and harmonious together.

The original, which I call *Transformation*, feels like energy being emitted and displaced as a bird takes flight. It's curious how two such different images came from the same painting. But the first one had to be what it was to create the second transformation. This painting was done for a hardworking entrepreneur who has a very kind and loving energy.

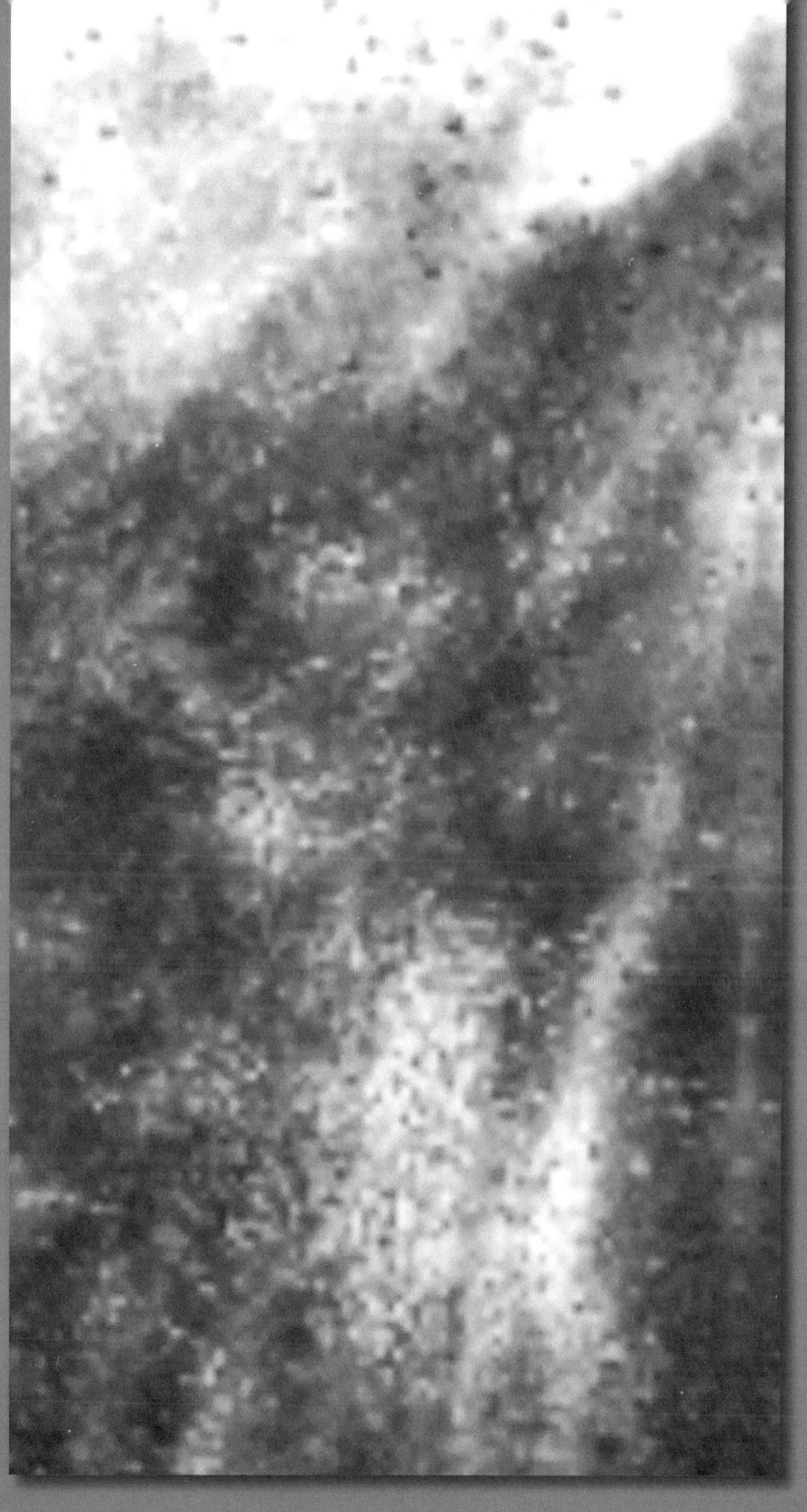

Energy of a Space

WATERCOLOR ON ART PAPER

I created this painting to explore the source of the uneasy feelings I experienced in a meeting space, which was located in an archdiocese building. I'll leave the interpretation up to you of what you see in the mirrored painting. Pay attention to the layers of images, as well as the dark robes. Even the dark energy seems to have a glow of light behind it.

Winged Dragon

OIL ON ART PAPER

The winged creature in this image emerges from the deep blue emotional base into an energetic orange and appears to be wearing an armored mask. Don't we all wear masks of some sort to present to the world only what we think it can handle of us? Is that mask what is holding us back from our true expression and the satisfaction of being seen for who we are? The ideal situation is to be the same person no matter who you're talking to ... authentic. I believe the bird is coaxing this person to lose the mask and take wing. Heal the damaged parts and set yourself free.

I painted it for a fiery redhead who did not embrace the power and magnificence this image portrays.

Spotted Warriors

INK ON RAW CANVAS

This painting has a lot of textures. The middle area of the mirrored version shows me angels and a female warrior goddess on the shoulders of her champion, who seems to be flexing his muscles.

After two years, I placed the canvas across from my bed only to wake up one morning to see the bigger image looking back at me. I wasn't ready or able to see it before. I was surprised and a little taken aback by what I saw.

Bound Hearts

ACRYLIC ON ART PAPER

Bound Hearts came out of a desire to paint a soul painting for a friend's birthday; while it was well received by the guests at the party, he felt much too exposed and was upset that his personal life was shared. That's proof it really did speak to him.

I see a beautiful representation of a human experience of love, complete with two hearts encased in rib cages in an almost X-ray-like image.

Only some people are open to sharing what's revealed.

A Bridge to the Other

OIL ON ART PAPER

Imagine, if you will, a client wanting a soul painting, and what she gets is what looks like a tree grounded in a dark blue emotional base, with spring colors of green—the heart chakra—and a bright sun. The orange is related to the sacral or second chakra, connected to creativity and childhood issues, and being either the Empress/Emperor in your life versus being the Martyr.

When mirrored, we get another picture. The tree has a twin, and a bridge between the two is visible. I see a solid, masculine-looking character under the bridge with a crown. I later discovered my client does have a twin, and they are on the outs. She wasn't ready to embrace what her painting was showing her. I hope they have found a way, or a bridge, back to each other. My client has a much-loved orange cat, and he also showed up in the picture.

This painting makes me think of finding a way across to another being. Communication, compassion, and forgiveness are required to develop a bridge to the other.

The roots of the bridge are sunk in a watery emotional abyss. Under that bridge is a crowned figure representing the tremendous responsibility that comes with authority. Being in the water, I thought of him as Poseidon. Such a powerful figure may represent the need for wisdom, humility, and fairness in showing power in the world using a higher state of consciousness and spiritual enlightenment.

Always look for the deeper meaning of what these experiences are teaching you. When you can come away with a deeper meaning, you're complete.

Struggles

ACRYLIC ON ART PAPER

This artwork was created for a client. The shadowy foundation, with the heart visible in the external world, conveys strong intentions radiating outward, yet there's an internal struggle hidden from the world's view. The basement or bottom of the piece, to me, represents the past and some trauma that is still affecting their life. Someone's will and ego (yellow third chakra) was pushed onto this person.

The face is a dark spirit, in my opinion, and is still a part of this person's life, at least in memory. The person who came out of the experience is showing love to the best of their ability in the outer world. And without a doubt the struggle to come out of childhood trauma is real. Their past has definitely shaped the person they have become.

Roots and Wings

WATERCOLOR ON ART PAPER

This commissioned piece made the recipient feel validated by her guides. The original shows her with her uplifted hairdo and her outgoing, open mouth, which she felt was how her guides initially saw her. Then, as she meditated on her painting, she also saw the closed mouth. I think they love all of her just as she is. The characters she saw as a child in her room at night showed up in the mirrored version, which also reflects who she has become in this lifetime. Someone who gives the people she coaches roots and wings.

Spirit Mountain

WATERCOLOR ON ART PAPER

This painting evokes a sense of meditation. In Feng Shui, a mountain of this type relates to wisdom, spirituality, innovation, benefactors, and recognition. You can feel Source above in the radiant, creamy color, representing inner peace and promoting self-discovery.

The belly of the mountain is a deep
and complicated space.

Marilyn Monroe/
Representations of Spirit

WATERCOLOR ON ART PAPER

It's difficult to name, much less describe this piece. In the original, I see the face of a woman who reminds me of Marilyn Monroe energy. The mirroring process tells so many more stories.

The subsequent layers of mirroring created levels of characters within a very strong body. I recommend looking for the eyes. There are many layers of eyes, and each pair are attached to a character. Just like in a dream, our subconscious has a difficult time showing us what it needs to, so it creates representations of its message.

I see a few birds at the top of the mirrored version. Notice the wings and beaks. Wings symbolize divine protection, the soul's journey, spiritual ascension, and symbolic balance.

Purple Sage

OIL ON ART PAPER

Look toward the center of this painting and see a seated sage with a temple in his belly and a flame on his head. Flanking him are two mythical creatures forming the shape of a heart. The branches of the tree look like they rest on his shoulders in support. Every person I show this to sees different things. So don't worry if you don't see what I do. Your personal experience is accurate as well.

Taking Flight One

OIL ON ART PAPER

In creating paintings for others, I enter a meditative state, linking my Higher Self with theirs to discern any messages they wish to communicate. I observe the colors that appear behind my closed eyelids and use these as the palette for my artwork. Occasionally, a sense of incompleteness persists, prompting me to continue working on the painting. This process unfolded in these and the subsequent mirrored images, where minor adjustments unveiled entirely new characters showing dimensions of the individual's spirit.

Taking Flight Two

OIL ON ART PAPER

I took a photo of the image at one point, before continuing to paint, without looking to see what the mirrored version of that initial image was. So two versions created different mirrored images of the same painting. The subject is quite a complicated fellow, don't you think?

Animal Spirit

WATERCOLOR ON ART PAPER

This painting was done for a man who likes getting things done, a person who aims to protect those he loves. He is very creative and quite intense. His painting contains a llama, a wolf, a baboon, a bat, and a bear, shown in the separate pictures. Some of them create different animals when rotated.

You may find others that I have not. What does what you have found mean? You may find a message that you need right now.

Accidental Angels

WATERCOLOR ON ART PAPER

These angels are actually the same painting at two different points in time. The first one happened as the watercolor was drying. The second one is the result of my affecting it afterward. With watercolor, any small artistic adjustment can create a huge change in the final work. So, in order to save the painting, what came about is a new angel. I think they're showing me that my angels are present in my life.

What a wonderful reassurance and
comfort to know I can ask them for help
when I'm confused or frightened.

Intuition

ACRYLIC ON ART PAPER

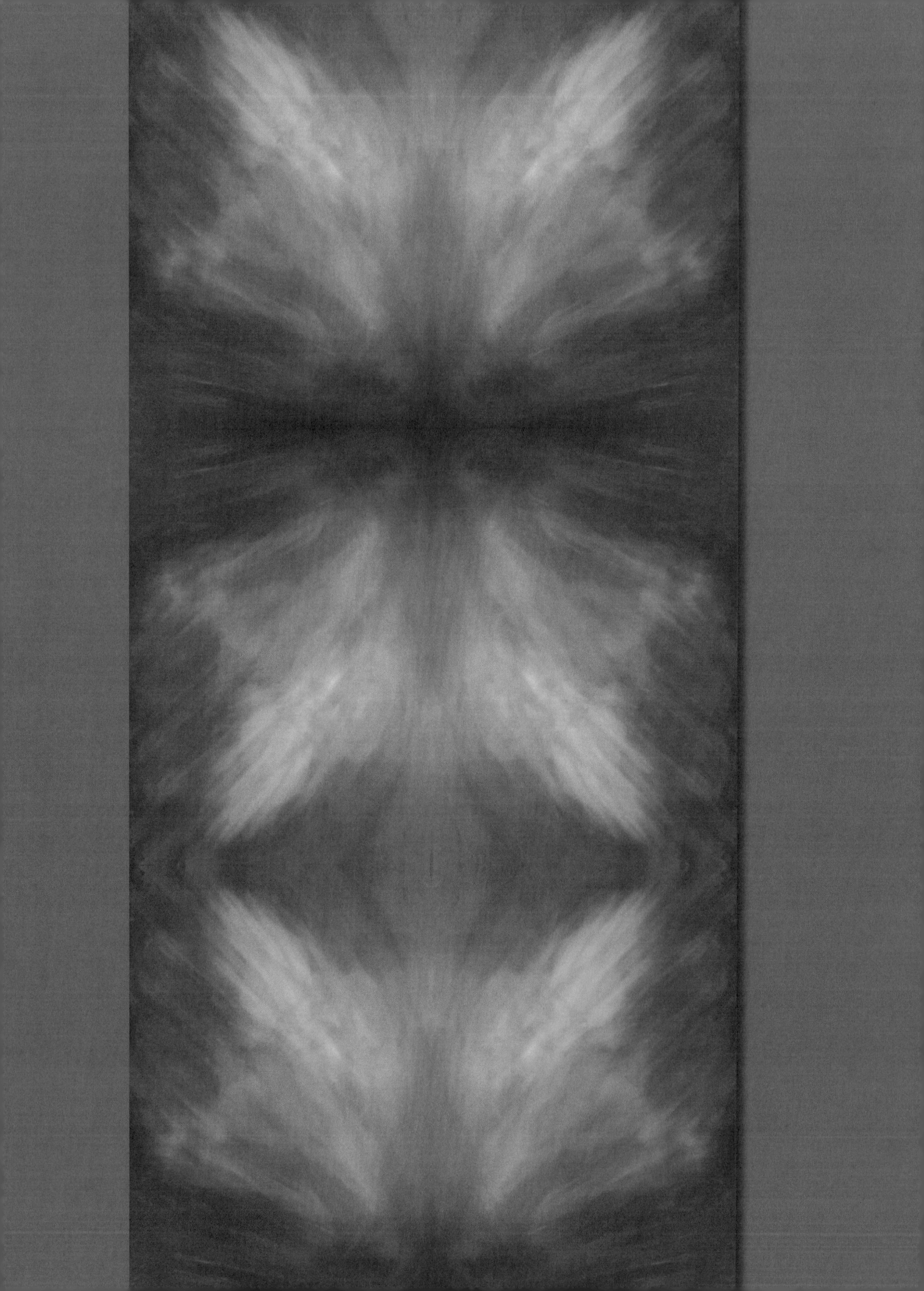

What becomes very obvious to me in this image is the third eye and the mouth. A light definitely highlights these areas.

What message do you get while viewing these images? A reminder to see, with our inner eye, the truth of any situation, perhaps? To look inward? When I say look inward, I'm saying using the inner eye to do a scan of the inside of your body. Where do you feel dis-ease?

The closed mouth is saying, "Listen," and not just blurt out the first thing you're thinking … or possibly that is what it's telling me! Not every situation can be fixed using words; however, a lot of problems begin with them!

Emergence /
What's Under the Bed?

ACRYLIC ON CANVAS

Emergence was done in the spring of 2020, the same week as George Floyd's passing, and reflects the energy of a time when we all needed our protectors and guides. I used a hotel key card to paint with. The dynamic image seems to represent the birth of a new situation. In the upper right corner is what appears to be a person wearing African tribal regalia calling out in protest.

I call the mirrored version *What's Under the Bed?* because at the lower end of the painting, there seems to be a crouching animal with two shifting faces, ready to lunge. Above this, layers of formidable characters appear, particularly one with large ears and another very large figure with broad shoulders. These multiple forms seem mythical to me. I imagine them in a storyline. Would a pandemic be the creature lurking below, ready to pounce, or is it a protector there to keep me safe?

Little Owl / Resilience

ACRYLIC ON CANVAS

I played with oil paint and a brush as well as wide packing tape, to see what effect it would create. When I finished, I noticed a little bird in the middle of the painting. A tiny owl, perhaps?

It was the spring of 2020, the beginning of COVID-19, and the painting is apropos of my life at that time in so many ways. The white owl relates to transformation and a reminder that nothing lasts forever. It looks like it may have new nest material in its mouth. I was staying in a temporary cabin on Lake Coeur d'Alene in Idaho, and my time there was coming to a close.

When mirrored, there is an entirely new story. I see characters inside of a large ape-wizard figure, who is wearing a robe with flowing sleeves. An owl flanks both sides of this figure. There is a black woman with slanted eyes wearing a long dress in the lower center and she has what may be an animal above her head.

Around the world, apes have been regarded as symbols of strength and resilience, wisdom, communication, and as guides and protectors. Apes are often associated with intuition and a strong connection to the natural world. As you change the focus in your gaze, you will notice shifting images that may have meaning to you.

The Kaleidoscope

OIL ON CANVAS

I love when I walk into high-end gift stores and see beautifully carved kaleidoscopes on the counter to try. The colored glass they use inside is especially beautiful.

You may have had a toy kaleidoscope—a small object you could look through and turn to reveal constantly changing shapes, colors, and patterns. No images were ever the same. With one little turn of the mechanism, everything shifts, making a new, unique image each time and for each person who looks through it. The same viewfinder hole, the same small, colored stones, pieces of glass, plastic, or even confetti—and a completely different view.

This reminds me of humans with our cells and molecules and thoughts and patterns. The same building blocks are inside of each of us. Yet all it takes is a little turn of our perspective, then we get a totally new, beautiful outcome.

Sometimes when I look into a kaleidoscope everything appears dull until I remember I need to turn to the light in order to truly appreciate what it has to offer. Often, we are stuck in our lives in the same way. We are hardened in our belief system and unwilling to shift our perspective. How often might we only need to add light to situations we encounter? Simply by facing a new direction, everything brightens. Adding light to a situation helps us see the good where it exists. There's always some good in a bad situation, as well as bad in a good one, the same way a yin/yang symbol has a little of the other color in it.

Are you able to rearrange your thoughts, words, and actions to create a new picture with just one or two shifts of perspective, thereby seeing the situation in a new light and seeing new possibilities open to you? The possibilities are always there.

There is a reason only one person can look through a kaleidoscope at a time—only you can change your picture. Others will watch your reaction to it, making them smile and want to see what you see. So, you carefully put the kaleidoscope in front of their eye and wait. It's difficult not to be discouraged if they don't have the same reaction as you. Yet your life is yours and your perspective is truly unique, as theirs is as well.

I've shared with you these images and what I've seen in them. I've offered you the kaleidoscope, hoping you too will feel a sense of the enchantment and wonder I have felt. I cannot dictate or anticipate what you will see, but I know your insight and perspective are beautiful and necessary.

Go ahead. Take another look.

Colorful One

OIL ON ART PAPER

Colorful Two

OIL ON ART PAPER

Block Original

OIL ON ART PAPER

Block Turtle

OIL ON ART PAPER

Blocks Dog

OIL ON ART PAPER

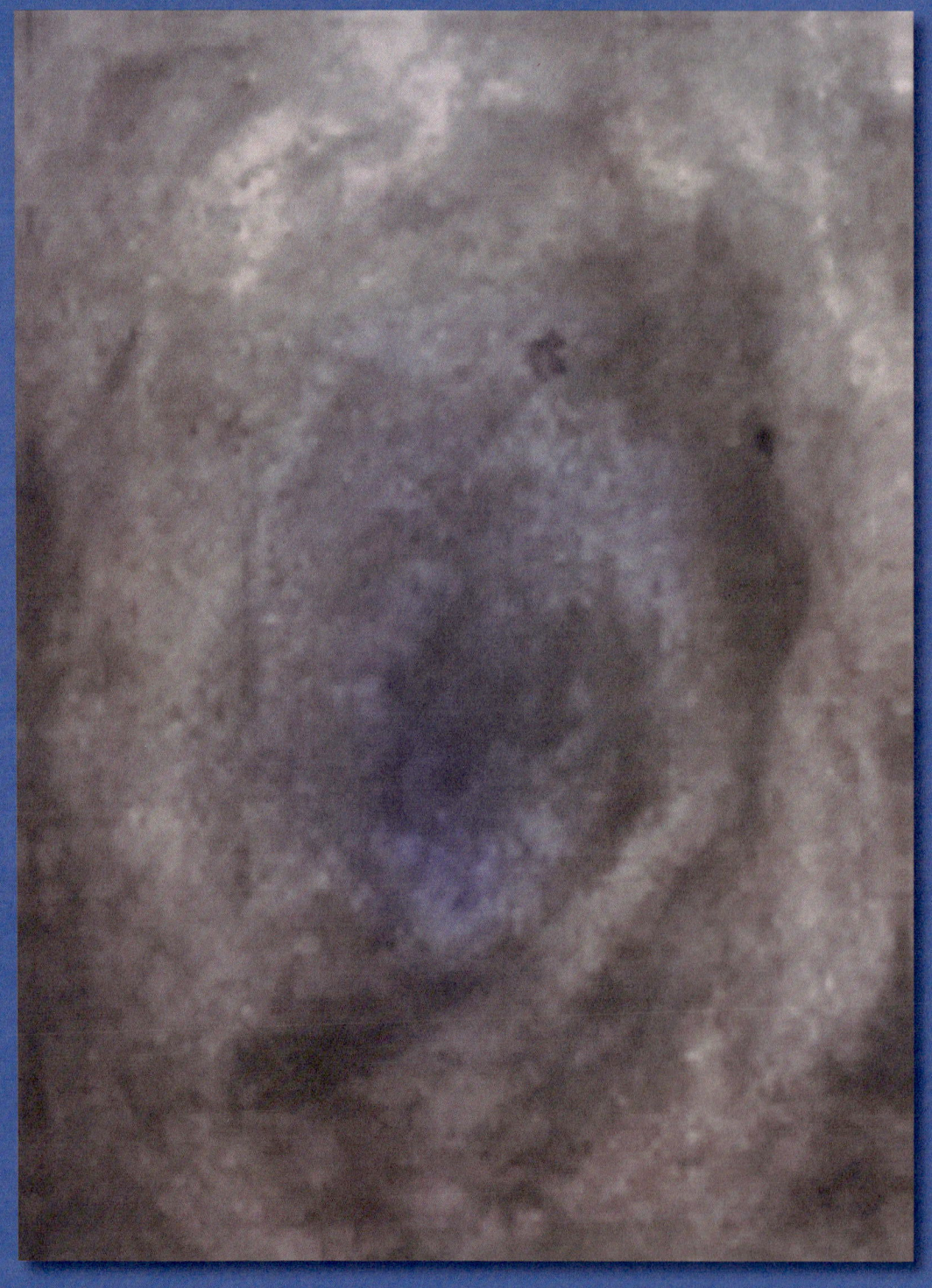

Blue Eyes

WATERCOLOR ON ART PAPER

Acknowledgments

I HAVE FAMILY AND FRIENDS TO THANK in the process of this art coming to this book ... some willing, and some perhaps unwilling victims! Becky is the industrious daughter who uploaded my art to a fabric design website, discovering the pattern, so to speak. My son Brian is more of a "You can do this, Mom, figure it out!" while also technical support, helping when he could kind of guy. Child number three, Evan, loves the originals and sees no need to go further. "Keep painting, Mom!" I love you all more than you can ever know.

Not to forget my mother, who said, "Nobody's going to buy them, anyway." Thanks, Mom, they already have. And my sisters who said, "How did you do this? How did Grandpa show up in the painting?" No exorcism necessary, thank you very much!

To my Fundamentals of Design instructor, the late Gerta Hess, who taught us these rules on the first day of class. The last one especially helped me more than you can know: "Four Rules For Life: Show up. Pay attention. Tell the truth. Don't be attached to the results." ⬩Angeles Arrien

Naomi Kamla was a great inspiration and support for making me believe I could do this process for not only myself, but for others as well. Members of my Mastermind group in Denver volunteered to be the guinea pigs and let me paint their spirits. Their names shall remain anonymous to protect their identities and spirits.

Then the various friends who encouraged me to keep painting. And finally, put them into a book to share. Saying, the world loves this stuff, go for it! You know who you are.

Then there's my faithful furry friend, Woogy, a wheaten and mini poodle mix (a whoodle) who makes sure I get out to enjoy nature and get those walks in.

To Polly Letofsky, thanks for shining your light onto this self-publishing path. To my editor Alexandra O'Connell, who I'm so grateful for—thanks for bringing out the best and prompting what was needed. And to my interior and cover designer, Victoria Wolf, thank you for displaying the art so beautifully.

To the angels, guides, and spirits who were so insistent in making sure I put this book to print to show others what they also had working for and loving them, shutting doors I wasn't meant to be on, and nudging me in the right direction. I'm so looking forward to discovering what's next!

About the Artist

While the person applying paint on the substrate may have been Janet Miller, she can't really take responsibility for the outcome as that was totally not her intent when she set about painting.

She was a conduit for what came through her. From her practice, she totally understands other authors and artists who believe they downloaded the information they wrote down or discovered. We are left to do our best to decipher what has come through and birth it into the world.

Janet has been working in the field of interior design for more than two decades. She has owned her own design business, enhancing the lives of many people through her ability to create a warm and comfortable living environment. Janet's easy-to-work-with style is in tune with her clients and represents their vision for their home or business.

Because of Janet's sensitivity to the energy around her, she has become a Reiki Master/Teacher and Feng Shui consultant, as well as studying the effects of color on human life in order to better help her clients.

Janet now lives in Montana, near two of her three children and their families. You can find her and more of her work at www.janilyn.net or email her at janet@janilyn.net.